2wice

FORMAL

From debutantes and brides, to ballerinas and dandies, formality is expressed through clothing as much as behavior. The rituals and artifacts that we refer to as "formal" share an element of theatricality, an attitude that encourages us to be our most dignified, civilized selves. This sense of theater can reach extremes, as Andrew Solomon describes in his essay on the extravagant fashions of the dandy. Formal clothing can also become a kind of masquerade, as evidenced by Catherine Smith and Cynthia Greig in their contribution on the recurrence of women in tuxedos over the last century. In the realm of dance, ballet represents the height of formality. In our photographic portfolios we represent this tradition as it is passed down from one generation to the next. Bart Cook and Maria Calegari, former members of the New York City Ballet and now répétiteurs for the Balanchine Trust, are followed by Albert Evans, Janie Taylor and Sébastien Marcovici, three current members of the New York City Ballet. Finally, photographer Tina Barney's stately group portraits show how traditions persist, despite the cultural changes that root us in the present. Our goal with this issue was to represent how our ideas of formality—while rooted in history—continue to inform the way we represent ourselves through fashion, dance, photography, and art. PATSY TARR AND ABBOTT MILLER

JANIE TAYLOR AND SÉBASTIEN MARCOVICI, PHOTOGRAPH BY CHRISTIAN WITKIN

TABLE OF CONTENTS

6   MAGNUM   64   PETER THE GREAT   94   BOLERO

20   DANDYISM   72   LOVE IN 3/4   100   SPEAKING BALLET

34   WOMEN IN TUXEDOS   84   RE-DRESSING POWER   108   FORMAL SITTING

60   DESCENT   90   DANCE WITH ME

SCRAMBLE FOR AFRICA BY YINKA SHONIBARE, 2000–2003
14 FIGURES, 14 CHAIRS, TABLE, COMMISSIONED BY THE MUSEUM FOR AFRICAN ART, NEW YORK
COURTESY THE ARTIST AND STEPHEN FRIEDMAN GALLERY, LONDON

PLATES AND FIGURES

16	FIG. 1–3	42	PLATE I. — V.	58	FIG. 12
32	FIG. 4–5	48	PLATE VI. — XI.	68	FIG. 13–14
40	FIG. 6–7	54	FIG. 8–11	114	FIG. 23–24

BERMUDA, ELLIOTT ERWITT, 1953

MAGNUM

There are two images of Magnum Photos Inc., the fabled cooperative photo agency, founded in the spring of 1947 over a lunch at the Museum of Modern Art in New York. In one, Robert Capa stands in a landing craft in GI uniform awaiting the start of the D-Day invasion, his camera slung around his neck and a cigarette clenched in his hand. In the other, the same Capa, neatly coiffed and wearing a crisp suit and tie, smiles a seductive, roué grin across a restaurant table of empty glasses. Capa, the combat photographer, epicure, and bon vivant, was the principle founder of Magnum, the socially committed, left-leaning conscience of photo-journalism whose name is Latin for great and English for a large bottle of wine.

Magnum's oscillation between the poles of social upheaval and comfortable society is inscribed in its beginnings and has been remarked upon ever since. That founding lunch, after all, was made possible by the Rockefellers' commitment to high culture. So it is no surprise that besides photographing war refugees, Holocaust survivors, tribal peoples, and peasants, Magnum photographers have documented the wealthy, tuxedo-and-gown set of America's postwar years. These pictures are of formal gatherings and their preludes, but they are informal as images in the sense that those who made them are unnoticed. Presumably the photographers, too, were in formal wear. Whether this qualifies as collaboration with the enemy or as the kind of mufti that makes irony possible is the question. Its answer might be found in the apparent wardrobe malfunction that puts a slip below a debutante's knees, or in the tight-lipped toast of ladies hanging on to beauty by a thread, or in the vacancy of the elegant dancer who grasps a bunny mask through the eye. The eyes of Magnum photographers are penetrating, too. ANDY GRUNDBERG

ABOVE

BLACK BOURGEOISIE DEPUTANTE BALL AT
THE WALDORF-ASTORIA, NEW YORK CITY,
EVE ARNOLD, 1964

LEFT

A SOCIETY WOMAN TRIES ON A BALL GOWN AT
BERGDORF-GOODMAN IN PREPARATION FOR
THE METROPOLITAN OPERA'S GALA OPENING,
NEW YORK CITY, BURT GLINN, 1951

FAR LEFT

LINDY GUINESS AND THE EARL OF SUFFOLK AT
THE BALL FOR THE DEBUT OF LINDY GUINESS,
BELVOIR CASTLE, ENGLAND, BURT GLINN, 1959

ABOVE
FANCY DRESS BALL, MONTE-CARLO, FERDINANDO
SCIANNA, 1968

RIGHT
OPENING OF THE CANNES FILM FESTIVAL, FRANCE,
HENRI CARTIER-BRESSON, 1953

FAR RIGHT
QUEEN CHARLOTTE'S BALL, LONDON, HENRI

TOP
HENRI CARTIER-BRESSON, 1957

ABOVE
DUKE OF RUTHLAND AT THE BALL FOR THE DEBUT OF LINDY GUINESS, BELVOIR CASTLE, ENGLAND, BURT GLINN, 1959

14

CANDICE BERGEN AT THE TRUMAN CAPOTE BLACK AND WHITE BALL, PLAZA HOTEL, NEW YORK CITY, ELLIOTT ERWITT, 1966

A BRIDE'S BOUQUET

"THE RADIANCE OF A TRULY HAPPY BRIDE IS SO BEAUTIFYING
THAT EVEN A PLAIN GIRL IS MADE PRETTY, AND A PRETTY ONE,
DIVINE."

fig. 1

ONCE UPON A TIME IN THE 1940S, A GIRL WHO LIVED IN A TOWER CALLED THE BERESFORD WOULD FROM TIME TO TIME LOOK OUT HER WINDOW AND GLIMPSE A YOUNG MAN IN AN ADJACENT TOWER. AND FROM TIME TO TIME, HE WOULD LOOK OUT HIS WINDOW AND GLIMPSE HER.

THEY WERE BOTH ATTRACTIVE AND UNATTACHED, AND SOMETIMES WENT OUT ON BLIND DATES, WHICH WAS WHAT PEOPLE DID BEFORE DIGITAL IMAGES AND E-MAIL. AND SO ONE AFTERNOON THEY FOUND THEMSELVES LOOKING AT EACH OTHER NOT OUT A WINDOW BUT ACROSS A TABLE, SET UP BY MARRIED FRIENDS—HE THE GROOM'S, SHE THE BRIDE'S—WHO NEVER GUESSED THEY HAD BEEN SEEING EACH OTHER, AFTER A FASHION, FOR QUITE A WHILE. YOU COULD SAY THEY MET CUTE.

fig.2

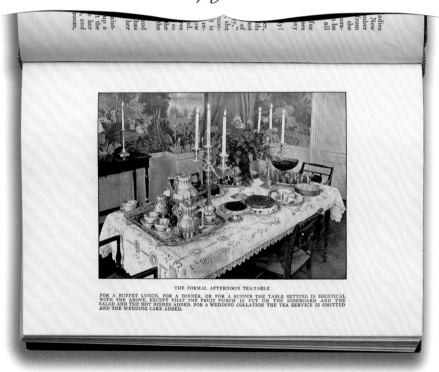

THE FORMAL AFTERNOON TEA-TABLE

FOR A BUFFET LUNCH, FOR A DINNER, OR FOR A SUPPER THE TABLE SETTING IS IDENTICAL WITH THE ABOVE, EXCEPT THAT THE FRUIT PUNCH IS PUT ON THE SIDEBOARD AND THE SALAD AND THE HOT DISHES ADDED. FOR A WEDDING COLLATION THE TEA SERVICE IS OMITTED AND THE WEDDING CAKE ADDED.

AFTER LUNCH, THE FOURSOME—THEIR INTRODUCERS WERE WITH THEM—WENT BACK TO HER PLACE, AND SHE AND HER MOTHER PLAYED FOUR-HAND PIANO, WHICH WAS NOT AN UNUSUAL ENTERTAINMENT IN MUSICALLY INCLINED HOUSEHOLDS OF THE DAY. NO ONE IS LEFT NOW TO REMEMBER WHETHER THE GROOM WORE HIS UNIFORM, BUT WE CAN BE SURE HER TURNOUT WAS IMPECCABLE.

THEY WERE MARRIED FROM HER PARENTS' APARTMENT, FROM WHICH SHE HAD FIRST SEEN HIM AND IN WHICH HE HAD FIRST SEEN HER. SHE WORE A GLEAMING WHITE GOWN WITH A SATIN SWEETHEART NECKLINE INSET IN A TRANSLUCENT BODICE THAT CAME RIGHT UP TO HER THROAT. HE WORE THE CRISP DRESS WHITES OF A LIEUTENANT IN THE UNITED STATES NAVY.

missing must unfailingly be sent for. The bride's mother gives her a last kiss, her bridesmaids hurry downstairs to have plenty of rice ready and to tell everyone below as they descend: "Here they come!" A passage from the stairway and out of the front door, all the way to the motor, is left free between two rows of eager guests, their hands full of rice. Upon the waiting motor the ushers have tied everything they can lay their hands on in the way of white ribbons and shoes and slippers.

"HERE THEY COME!"

At last the groom appears at the top of the stairs, a glimpse of the bride behind him. It surely is running the gauntlet! They seemingly count "one, two, three, go!" With shoulders hunched and collars held tight to their necks, they run through shrapnel of rice, down the stairs, out through the hall, down the outside steps, into the motor, slam the door, and are off!

The wedding guests stand out on the street or roadway looking after them for as long as a vestige can be seen—and then gradually disperse.

Occasionally young couples think it clever to slip out of the area-way, or over the roofs, or out of the cellar and across the garden. All this is supposed to be in order to avoid being deluged with rice and having labels of "newly wed" or large white bows and odd shoes and slippers tied to their luggage.

Most brides, however, agree with their guests that it is decidedly "spoil sport" to deprive a lot of friends—who have only their good luck at heart—of the perfectly legitimate enjoyment of throwing emblems of good luck after them. If one white slipper among those thrown after the motor lands right side up, on top of it, and stays there, greatest good fortune is sure to follow through life.

There was a time when the "going away carriage" was always furnished by the groom, and this is still the case if it is a hired conveyance. But nowadays when nearly everyone has a motor, the newly married couple—if they have no motor of their own—are sure to have one lent them by the family of one of them. Very often they have two motors and are met by a second car at an appointed place, into which they change after shaking themselves free of rice. The white ribboned car returns to the house, as well as the decorated and labeled luggage, which was all

fig.3

THEY WERE A PERFECT MATCH, AND THEIR WEDDING BUFFET, IN TURN, PERFECTLY MATCHED THEM. DRESSED IN WHITE, LIT BY STATELY CANDELABRA, TOPPED WITH A THREE-TIERED WHITE CAKE, THE TABLE EXPRESSED TO PERFECTION THE FORMAL STANDARD OF THEIR DAY.

BEFORE LONG THE BRIDE CHANGED INTO AN AFTERNOON DRESS, AND WITH HER WHITE GLOVES CLASPED IN HER LEFT HAND, SHE TOSSED HER BOUQUET FROM THE STAIRWAY THAT LED UP TO HER GIRLHOOD BEDROOM. THEN SHE TOOK THE GROOM'S ARM AND THEY RAN OFF INTO THEIR FUTURE, WHERE THEY LIVED HAPPILY, AND PROPERLY, EVER AFTER.

DANDYISM

ANDREW SOLOMON

LET US CONSIDER THE WORD DANDYISM.
SOME USE THE WORD AS A EUPHEMISM FOR FOPPISH
EXHIBITIONISM. OTHERS USE IT TO REFER TO A *FROIDEUR*
IN WHICH THE AFFECT OF THE SUBJECT IS SUBSUMED
BY A DEVOTION TO RIGOROUSLY CONTROLLED AND ALMOST
ASCETICALLY ELEGANT APPEARANCE.

There are ample questions posed by the two ideas. What is the purpose of men's clothing of style, be that style extravagant or controlled? What rules govern the wearing of men's clothing? And is the principle that informs the wild runway show of club gear the same as or different from the one that informs impeccable bespoke tailoring? And perhaps most mysteriously, what is it that a dandy adds to his clothing? For Jules Barbey d'Aurevilly, whose nineteenth-century treatise on Beau Brummell remains the single most important text on dandyism, wrote to Thomas Carlyle in 1845, "Dandyism is…not a suit of clothes walking about by itself! On the contrary, it is the particular way of wearing these clothes which constitutes dandyism."

The mainstream view for most of the last century was that there was nothing attractive about evident self-consciousness in a man's dress. Our standards of desire revolved around basics—the James Dean white T-shirt, beat-up jacket, and old Levis, or the well-pressed white shirt smelling starchily of freshness, rep tie, and classic suit (not a "reinterpretation" of the

classic suit, but that suit itself). How did we come to the idea that real men shouldn't wear fancy clothing—which reached its epitome in the 1950s—and how is it that we have begun to move past that notion with the advent of men's designer clothes? Anne Hollander, in *Sex and Suits*, writes, "There are new eyes for the gaudy old devices that once clothed male power before the modern era; the look of male sexual potency in the post-modern world is able to float free of those austere visions of masculinity that discredited any richness of fantasy." Gilles Lipovetsky, the hip French philosopher of fashion, acknowledged a few years ago that "after a long period of exclusion marked by the conservative dark suit, men are 'back in style.'"

This return to style has altered even looks that are intended to be above self-consciousness. The miner emerging from a mine may still be rather sexy to some people's way of thinking, and the senator wearing a suit nearly identical to his father's may still have an old-fashioned look of power, but for the rest of us, whatever we wear is deliberate, and so the

YOUNG DANDY, DIRECTOIRE PERIOD, CA. 1795
PRINT BY CARLE VERNET. GIANNI DAGLI ORTI/CORBIS

DANDY-STYLE HAT AND A SCALLOPED COAT, 1780
HISTORICAL PICTURE ARCHIVE/CORBIS

inherent sexiness of unconsidered modes of dress has pretty much vanished. "We may now find," Hollander writes, "the curious spectacle of a man privately at ease fifteen stories above the city street, sipping wine and reading Trollope in a warm room furnished with fragile antiques and Persian rugs, dressed in a costume suitable for roping cattle on the plains or sawing up lumber in the North woods." Can such a man think that his choice is somehow above fashion? The choices have simply become too manifest. You cannot spend your life in what you haven't chosen and aren't wearing, and if you've put on jeans to achieve a look, the look you have is of having achieved a look. What then? Once carefree authenticity is gone, the doors are flung wide open.

This recent revolution in male dress owes a great deal to feminism. As women took over work that had been the province of men and men accepted a participatory role in cooking and child-rearing, newly sensitive fellows began to wear facial expressions they had not worn before. By the mid-'80s, "healthy" fellows were supposed to cry and to admit

fear. Men could be depressed and could talk about it. At the same time that men's faces softened, their bodies hardened. The vanity of the physique was evidence of a compensatory hypermasculinity, and male preening was back. Maurizia Boscagli, in *Eye on the Flesh*, writes, "The superman wears his muscles as a suit, and the modern male body is a new costume of masculinity, a fashionable yet far-reaching style in clothing." If your face has emotion written on it and your body is a nexus of your pride, then you have become the sum of deliberate and expressive parts.

But there is another piece here. In *Rising Star: Dandyism, Gender, and Performance in the Fin de Siècle*, Rhonda K. Garelick, a scholar of the mode, argues that the idea of celebrity is rooted in dandyism and that the dandyist sensibility must reemerge in our celebrity-oriented era. Garelick describes dandyism as "the artform of commodifying personality. It is itself the performance of a highly stylized, painstakingly constructed self; the dandy is a self-created, carefully controlled man whose goal is to create an

PORTRAIT OF CHARLES BAUDELAIRE, CA. 1860
STAPLETON COLLECTION/CORBIS

DANDY'S DRESSING ROOM, CA. 1900
HULTON-DEUTSCH COLLECTION/CORBIS

effect, bring about an event, or provoke a reaction in others; as a movement founded against nature, dandyism prizes perpetual, artificial youth and a reified immobilized self." This is quite a different matter from being well dressed. You may be well dressed in a pair of corduroys and a crewneck sweater. The dandy wears clothing that takes over from other manifestations of self. This clothing does what conversation might do, or what accomplishment might do, or what song or dance or gesture or glance might do. Dress has become increasingly important in a society in which other social markers have weakened. The man made by the clothes that make the man is an intensely personal, passionate collector whose habits belie his fragility.

Baudelaire said that dandies were like women in their cultivation of artifice. Barbey wrote, "To *appear* to be is *to be* for Dandies." How much does our society reward appearing even at the expense of being? A well-educated man gives the impression of having read a great many books he has never opened. A dandy gives the impression of looking better than

he is: the appearing is sufficient. Roland Barthes, certainly a study in male vanity, declared, "The dandy combines the indolent and the fashionable with the pleasure of causing surprise in others while never showing any himself. He is the expert on the fleeting pleasures of the moment."

The seventeenth century saw men's wish for modish clothing as a reflection of their taste for constant novelty, especially sexual novelty (as opposed to women's natural tendency toward constancy). In Restoration comedy, men's conversation about their own clothing became a symbol for their licentiousness. "Nat that I pretend to be a beau," says Lord Foppington in Vanburgh's *The Relapse*, "but a man must endeavour to look wholesome, lest he make so nauseous a figure in the side box, the ladies should be compelled to turn their eyes upon the play." Self-conscious label-awareness was suddenly manifest at this time as well. Sir Fopling in Etherege's *Man of Mode* wears only French clothing and can tell who made each thing: "The suit? Barroy. The garniture?

PORTRAIT OF GEORGE BRUMMEL
BETTMANN/CORBIS

JOHN BARRYMORE AS BEAU BRUMMEL, 1923
PHOTOGRAPH BY JOHN SPRINGER. JOHN SPRINGER COLLECTION/CORBIS

Le Gras. The shoes? Piccar. The periwig? Chedreux." It sounds horribly like a social climber on the next-to-last flight of the Concorde. Men's "novel" clothing is oriented not so much toward its effect on others and its power to seduce as toward the pleasure of change among people of insatiable appetite. "If we had the liberty," says Marwood in *The Way of the World*, "we shou'd be as weary of one Set of Acquaintance…as we are of one suit." Held as men are by the conventions that limit the number of lovers they may have, they are allowed, at least, to seek and find change constantly in their clothing, and so to live in "civilization." But none of these men supposes that the clothing determines his fate; it is, like male promiscuity before the clap, an innocent foolish pleasure.

Already in 1642, however, Reverend Thomas Fuller had observed that "good clothes open all doors." The full import of this assertion became clear only with the advent of Beau Brummell in the late eighteenth century. Brummell, our greatest exemplar of dandyism, was the son of a civil servant. Through

the sheer force of his style, and without any particular wisdom or even wit, he became the closest friend of the Prince Regent and the most sought-after member of his society. He was history's most successful *arriviste*. Barbey wrote that he "saw instinctively that the day of aristocracy was over and that the day of gentility had arrived." To appear aristocratic was more important than to be aristocratic. Brummell expressed his gentility in dress. William Maginn, editor of the Regency journal *Fraser's Magazine*, wrote in Brummell's time, "There are *gentlemen* of two sort; the natural, and the tailor-made." George Walden in an essay on Brummell describes the essence of classical dandyism: "the dandy's stance of indolent superiority not just over the masses, but over all comers." The aristocracy aspired to copy Brummell, whose "terrible independence," Baudelaire wrote, "proclaimed a subversive disregard" for class privileges. Dandyism, in Baudelaire's view, was "a new kind of aristocracy, all the more difficult to break down because established on the most precious, the most indestructible faculties, on

MAX BEERBOHM, 1908
PHOTOGRAPH BY ALVIN LANGDON COBURN. HULTON-DEUTSCH
COLLECTION/CORBIS

HONORE DE BALZAC
MICHAEL NICHOLSON/CORBIS

the divine gifts that neither work nor money can give." He said, "Dandyism is the last burst of heroism in the decadent period."

Beau Brummel insisted that one's clothing should never attract attention; indeed, he often said that "the severest mortification which a gentleman could incur was to attract observation in the street by his outward appearance." Byron said of him that there was "a certain exquisite propriety" in his clothes, and Max Beerbohm wrote of "the utter simplicity of his attire" and "his fine scorn for accessories." As Carter Ratcliffe notes in a recent essay, he intended the initiated to see his invisibility. Thomas Carlyle's passionate treatise against dandyism, *Sartor Resartus*, said that the dandy "is a Clothes-wearing Man, a Man whose trade, office, and existence consists in the wearing of clothes." Such a dandy wants only to be "a visual object, or a thing that will reflect rays of light. Your silver or your gold…he solicits not; simply the glance of your eyes…. [D]o but look at him, and he is contented." Carlyle said of the dandy that "a 'Divine Idea of Cloth' is born with him; and

this…will express itself outwardly, or wring his heart asunder with unutterable throes." Fine clothing speaks on behalf of those who wear it; it saves the need for introductions and verbal captions. Balzac, the greatest of French dandies, wrote in 1832, "In making himself a dandy, a man becomes a piece of boudoir furniture, an extremely ingenious mannequin." If you put enough effort into your clothing, you need not put effort into anything else. "The sense of being well dressed," the dandy and writer Thomas Dunn English observed a hundred years ago, "gives a feeling of inward tranquillity which religion is powerless to bestow."

There is an intrinsic coldness here. Maurice Barrès, the turn-of-the-century novelist and politician, wrote, "What worries me about the position of the dandy and has kept me apart from them is the disguised Puritanism, the *noli me tangere*—you abstract yourself from life, from its stains and failures. In the end, I prefer to roll in the mud with others." And Cyril Connolly noted some fifty years later, "Dandyism is

KING CHARLES I
BETTMANN/CORBIS

KING EDWARD VII DRESSED FOR CORONATION
HULTON-DEUTSCH COLLECTION/CORBIS

capitalist, for the Dandy surrounds himself with beautiful things and decorative people and remains deaf to the call of social justice. As a wit, he makes fun of seriousness, as a lyricist he exists to celebrate things as they are, not to change them." Ratcliffe says that "the dandy's stillness is not the rigidity of one who strains against the weight of a monolithic bourgeoisie. The dandy is not a revolutionary…. He seeks nothing, and does next to nothing…permitting none of [his] behavior to serve any purpose save the maintenance of his frozen equipoise." "The most important relationship for the classical dandy," Garelick writes, "is that between himself and the inanimate world. Striving to become an art object, the dandy dehumanizes himself in order to create his social spectacle." The clothing does objectify you; it frees you from the burden of your complex reality, and gives you the pleasant grandeur of the physical art object, an amalgam of fully external metaphors.

Until the seventeenth century, men dressed as elaborately as possible and did not hide their vanity.

The public sense of clothing as privilege for men existed in the ancient world, then reached another apotheosis in the Italian Renaissance. Glamour was glamorous for men. And then it all fell apart—like so much else—during the English Civil War. Dreary old Oliver Cromwell introduced drab dress, and Royalist Cavaliers wore fancy-dandy doublets and hose to mark their support of the Crown. During the Restoration, Charles II launched the suit, and with it the new social order; it is no coincidence, as the great innovator and Savile Row tailor Hardy Amies has pointed out, that the beheading of Charles I marked the end of both the divine right of kings and the doublet and hose.

But why was men's self-decoration curtailed while women's remained rich and opulent? Once more, the answer lies in politics. Women's clothing has been essentially a French phenomenon, with all other nations copying the French model—and France excelled at decoration. Men's dress has been English, with Anglomania appearing in France, Germany, and even Italy. The basic reasons are

THE ACTOR ICHIKAWA MONNOSUKE II, CA. 1780
BROOKLYN MUSEUM OF ART. MUSEUM COLLECTION FUND

THE ACTOR SAKATA HANGORO, CA. 1780
BROOKLYN MUSEUM OF ART. MUSEUM COLLECTION FUND

simple. French clothing (pre-1789) was designed for courtiers living primarily at court. Magna Carta's democratizing effect meant that the British ruling classes spent most of their time on their own estates. When they came to court, they came on horseback and were often dressed in riding costume—which was not necessary for members of the less free French court. In the seventeenth and eighteenth centuries, Englishmen would often "come dirty"—in just what they'd worn to ride up to London—for social functions or even official occasions. The French courtiers, who envied the English their freedom, associated this pragmatism with self-determination. The age-old trappings of power—the gold of kings—came to be associated with the oppressive court and its petty intrigues, and plain clothing for men became a symbol of power. The original forms of English "dirty" dress survive in men's fashions today: the jackets we wear in a normal suit are based on the construction of early riding coats, vented to accommodate a horse; and the reason, for example, that men's coats and jackets button to the left is that

left-closure facilitates drawing a sword with your right hand. Proust observed that the most elegant men in the world were Frenchmen who bought their clothes in England. Barbey maintains that dandyism is at base a British tendency, that Brummell could never have been born of the French system.

Adolf Loos, writing in 1898, observed, "The dandies in every city look different." The same may be said of every time. Baudelaire wrote of dandies throughout history—Caesar, Catiline, and Alcibiades—and across cultures—he referred especially to American Indians done up in feathers. Japanese dandyism reached its apotheosis in *iki*, or Edo chic. Popular between the mid-seventeenth century and the mid-nineteenth, it was the style of pleasure-seekers. The Tokugawa shogunate's sumptuary laws were full of loopholes, and *iki* was the exploitation of those loopholes, realized by those with much money but imperfect social position. Michael Dunn has described it: "The *ch'nin* would line their clothing, restricted by code to cotton or plain silk, with sumptuous materials. Rather than

MAURICE BARRYMORE
PHOTOGRAPH BY SARONY, BETTMANN/CORBIS

THE DUKE OF WINDSOR
CONDÉ NAST ARCHIVE/CORBIS

displaying the bold and brightly colored robes favored by the nobility, *iki* connoisseurs promoted the fashion of subdued colors and small, geometric stencil patterns that, on close inspection, were as fine as the most elaborate court costumes. Accessories imitated lowly materials with a highly skilled deployment of lacquer and inlay techniques." The great philosopher of *iki* was Kuki Shūzō. He said, "Once you have set eyes on the vague traces of warm and sincere tears behind a bewitching, lightly-worn smile, you will have been able to grasp the manifestation of *iki* for the first time. Perhaps the resignation in *iki* is a mood produced by over-ripeness and decadence." Could those words not have come from des Esseintes, the ultimate dandy of literature, who replaced Brummell's emotional vacuity with a supercilious nostalgia and world-weary refinement?

While *iki* was reaching its height in Japan, dandyism bubbled up in the West. What had once been the path for a social aspirant became the province of royalty. Queen Victoria wrote irritably of the man who would

be Edward VII, "Unfortunately, he took no interest in anything but clothes, and again clothes. Even when out shooting he was more occupied with his trousers than with the game." The Duke of Windsor, the great dandy of the twentieth century, broke down the tyranny of formal dress. George V wrote to him, "From the various photographs of you which have appeared in the papers I see that you wear turn-down collars in white uniform, with collar and black ties. I wonder whose idea that was, as anything more unsmart I never saw." Such innovation was the prerogative of royalty. The great bourgeoisie has always been excluded from the world of dandyism, for the drab suit has been their triumph.

Gilles Lipovetsky has caused a stir in the academy with *The Empire of Fashion*, which has assumed a sort of celebrity trendiness on American campuses. Lipovetsky proposes that clothing does not so much reflect as determine the times. He maintains that democracy required this century's changes in fashion, which are the cause rather than the result of liberality. This radical idea of the importance of

NOEL COWARD, 1936
BETTMANN/CORBIS

THE DUKE OF WINDSOR
BETTMANN/CORBIS

fashion has long been part of the dandyist credo. Laurence Stern once said that "the ideas of a clean-shaven man are not those of a bearded man," and Beau Brummell said, "Actions are never anything but the consequences of our toilette." The radical Afro-American poet Amiri Baraka said in the 1960s that "Ideology and style are the same thing." Kemal Atatürk actually made the fez illegal in Turkey because he believed that depriving men of their funny hats would move them to industrialize. Peter the Great passed laws forcing his court into Western dress in order to bring about modernization.

Lipovetsky is not breaking new ground in suggesting that fashion is the origin of social structure. "Little remains to be said," he writes, "about the 'great male renunciation' of fashion and its connection with the rise of democracy and the bourgeoisie. The neutral, austere, sober masculine costume reflected the consecration of egalitarian ideology as the conquering bourgeois ethic of thrift, merit, and work. Costly aristocratic dress, a sign of celebration and pomp, was replaced by clothing that expressed the new social values of equality, economy, and effort. Since the nineteenth century, masculinity has been defined in contradistinction to fashion, to the ephemeral and the superficial."

With the abandonment of the suit as uniform, which is the ultimate nod from the privileged to the less privileged, men's clothing has taken on some of the liberalism of women's and has absorbed the idea of fantasy. "The clothing of both sexes," Lipovetsky observes, "is attuned to the mass happiness character-istic of consumer society." Men's attire, which for so long "precisely embodied the opposition between hedonistic values and technocratic values that characterizes capitalist societies," has given way to more individuated and ostentatious self-presentation. Following Lipovetsky to the logical extreme, one can say that male display is possible in a world less ambivalent than ever about capitalism and its pleasures. Taking up the themes put forward in the Restoration, one can also observe that the periods in which men have had the least freedom to dress (the Victorian, the '50s) are those in which society

PORTRAIT OF OSCAR WILDE
BETTMANN/CORBIS

JOHN GIELGUD, "THE IMPORTANCE OF BEING EARNEST"
BETTMANN/CORBIS

has worked hardest to contain male sexual appetite; and that when men are free to indulge in the search for erotic novelty, they are also permitted some leeway for sartorial innovation. The omnipresence now of looks that were once gay—jeans that fit, boots on people who aren't from Texas, white sneakers kept white, sweaters tucked in at the waist, not to mention color, even if it's mostly in polo shirts—demonstrates how steadily the gay sensibility in men's clothing has spread. The steadily expanding breadth of male self-expression through clothing since the Reagan era of the early '80s has coincided with increasing social acceptance of the male urge to promiscuity, and especially of gay men's pleasure in multiple partners. It is those same gay men who have multiple looks, for whom sexuality becomes a never-ending costume drama and costume a perpetual sexual game.

It would seem that in the heyday of the French court, extravagance of dress was not identified with any particular sexual orientation (though this was, of course, before the idea of an identity predicated on sexual orientation had gained currency). In the late nineteenth century, the men who wore fantastic clothing were often gay, and the clothing itself was indicative of attractions sometimes simply by its extravagance and sometimes in its particulars. During the period before the First World War, men in polite society who wore red neckties were signaling their homosexuality to one another. This connection between clothing and homosexuality, tasteful or otherwise, is not organic; it is indebted to the nineteenth-century aesthetes, and particularly to Oscar Wilde. Fashion is above all a game, and it works best when it is worn by people who are playing the game, rather than by those on whom the game is being played. Long before Pierre Cardin, Oscar Wilde staged an approximation of a men's fashion show. For the opening night of *Lady Windemere's Fan*, he arranged for a large number of men in the audience to wear green carnations in their lapels, and put a similar carnation in the lapel of the young male lead. "[The public] likes to be annoyed," Wilde observed. "A young man on the stage will wear a green carnation; people will stare at it and wonder. They

ROLAND BARTHES, 1978
PHOTOGRAPH BY SOPHIE BASSOULS, CORBIS/SYGMA

will then look round the house and see every here and there more and more little specks of mystic green. 'This must be some secret symbol,' they will say. 'What on earth can it mean?'" Wilde explained this plan of action to a friend, who wondered what it *did* mean. "Nothing whatever," Wilde replied, "but that is just what nobody will guess."

Wilde was one of the original fans both of subversion and of homoeroticism. Sometimes they coincided; sometimes they did not. His green carnations did have meaning; they meant that their wearers were in on the joke, and perhaps on the other transgressive jokes. Garelick writes that Wilde wanted "to co-opt his entire audience into entering a world of fetishized treasures and illicit desire." He contrived to fascinate people with something of no substance whatsoever. That is dandyism.

Cyril Connolly said in 1960, "The dandy is but the larval form of a bore." And yet the reality is that dandyism's cool self-assurance and visual spectacle have remained fascinating to us. Carlyle wrote, sarcastically, "May we not well cry shame on an ungrateful

world, that refuses even this poor boon; that will waste its optic faculty on dried Crocodiles, and Siamese twins; and over the domestic wonderful wonder of wonders, a live Dandy, glance with hasty indifference."

Roland Barthes has said that "reduced to a freedom to buy, dandyism could only suffocate and expire." There was a moment when that seemed to be true, perhaps, but it has passed. Barbey declared, "Dandies are as eternal as caprice. Humanity has as much need of their attractions as of its most imposing heroes, of its most austere grandeurs. We shall never have another dandy like Brummell, but people like him, whatever weight the world gives them, we can be sure there will always be, even in England." And, we might add, even in America.

fig.4

BENEATH THE BROOKLYN BRIDGE IN LIGHT MIST: BRIDES
AND GROOMS UNDER THE WATCHFUL EYE OF A
WEDDING DIRECTOR POSE FOR THEIR PHOTOS
OR WAIT THEIR TURN BEFORE THE LENS—NO NEED
FOR FILTERS TODAY, WHEN NATURE PROVIDES
THIS KIND FOG, CLOAKS ALL IN A BRIDAL
VEIL. THE ALBUMS WILL SHOW ONLY THE
COUPLES, THE CITY (NOTHING EXTRANEOUS).

fig.5

LUCKY THE BRIDE WHOSE GROOM HAS GIVEN HER
HIS JACKET. LUCKY THE RED UMBRELLA,
LIGHT AS THE BRIDES, COLORFUL AS THE
BOUQUETS (WET PETALS). PHIL TOLEDANO,
UNINVITED PHOTOGRAPHER, MARRIES
IT WITH HIS CAMERA, THE UNSEEN GROOM.

TEXT BY NANCY DALVA
PHOTOGRAPHS BY PHILLIP TOLEDANO, 2003

WOMEN IN TUXEDOS

CATHERINE SMITH AND CYNTHIA GREIG

LONG BEFORE MARLENE DIETRICH APPEARED AS A TUXEDO-CLAD BEAUTY IN THE 1930 FILM "MOROCCO," women gathered in front of the camera dressed in white ties and swallowtail coats, black dinner jackets and top hats, and starched white shirts with detachable wing collars. Nineteenth- and early-twentieth-century college women who attended all-female dances, participants in mock wedding ceremonies, lesbian couples, and other women who challenged traditional gender roles borrowed the often oversized formal attire of their brothers and fathers for festive occasions. Photographs reveal that while the rolled-up pants legs and long, baggy jackets betrayed the part-time nature of their transvestitism, other women— cross-dressers who passed as men, women's-rights leaders like Anna Dickinson, and actresses who appeared in breeches roles on the stage or as male impersonators like Vesta Tilley—clearly wore their own masculine clothing. According to a *New York Times* article, as early as 1884 women ordered tailor-made trousers and coats from a "fashionable Chestnut-street clothing house" in New York City: "This pair of trousers is for a very pretty little lady.... She is having three suits made. One is a

175 M MISS VESTA TILLEY. ROTARY PHOTO. E.C.

87 UNION SQR., N.Y.

Geissinger 1751-1753 Germantown Ave. Philadelphia.

CABINET CARDS AND PHOTO POSTCARDS, 1880–1910

ALL CARD IMAGES COURTESY CATHERINE SMITH

SIX WOMEN IN MEN'S ATTIRE, CABINET CARD, CA. 1880

knock-around suit, with a single-breasted sack [suit jacket]; another is a full-buttoned blue frock, with fancy lining, and the other suit has knickerbocker breeches, and is a very neat fit.... I don't know what this particular lady wanted with men's clothing, for we never ask." Undoubtedly, to escape taunting by the public and possibly arrest, these women wore their suits exclusively indoors, and most likely only in the presence of other women. Aside from a small number of reform-minded women like Dr. Mary Edwards Walker, only actresses who appeared on the stage dared to dress openly in male attire and then only during performances. Even as late as 1933, Marlene Dietrich was threatened with arrest when she appeared on the street in trousers.

During the last quarter of the nineteenth century as higher education became available to more women, young female college students had the opportunity to experiment with their attire while engaging in theatrical performances, sports, and social activities on campus. All-female formal dances, held at colleges like Wellesley and Smith, enabled a significant

number of the students to serve as escorts, dressed as elegant gentlemen. Though colleges forbade students to wear their male attire in public or to be photographed in it, many images of these same-sex couples survive. As a record of what Frances Willard called "two hearts in counsel, 'both of which are feminine,'" these images attest to the strong feelings many women held for one another. Photographs that captured mock wedding ceremonies with women in long gowns, serving as the bride and bridesmaids, and others in top hats and tuxedos as the groom and best man, have become testaments to these emotional bonds. Other such images reveal, often humorously, the resistance with which many women greeted their traditional social roles, while still others record what may be rehearsals for future relationships. As the nineteenth century came to a close and the fight for women's suffrage heated up, many more rebellious women dressed in masculine garb and stood before the camera. The proliferation of photographs of young trousered women in top hats or bowler hats, stiff collars and neckties, cutaway jackets or tuxedos,

DOCTOR MARY WALKER IN TUXEDO, 1912
BETTMANN/CORBIS

LA QUESTION EST POSEE : portera-t-on la jupe-pantalon en 1911 ? ?
Vue pour la première fois à la Comédie-Française, elle a indigné
le public. Aux Courses d'Auteuil, où nos couturiers l'ont ensuite
présentée, l'accueil a été plus gai, cette mode a beaucoup amusé
les habitués très intrigués par la nouveauté de ces dessous mys-
térieux.   ND Phot.

PARISIAN WOMEN WEARING PANTS, POSTCARD, 1911

often smoking or drinking, or staring boldly into the
camera, began to reflect an expanded role for women
in the world—one on an equal footing with men.
By 1925, women walked the Rue de la Paix and the
Avenue du Bois in jackets cut just like men's dinner
jackets. The *New York Times* reported, "Not content
with this daylight success in aping the appearance of
men, some advanced fashion makers are threatening
to carry masculine habit into the restaurant and
ballroom." One Parisian designer created a slimmed
skirt with "a feminine dinner coat complete with
silk lapels, stiff shirt front, wing collar, black tie and
pearl studs."

The uproar created by the female tuxedo (even
without the trousers!) in the first quarter of the twentieth century has given way to an erotic fascination
with androgyny and transvestitism. Crowds gathered
at the Rockland Palace Casino in Harlem to see
women dancing in tuxedos and men in gowns at the
annual Hamilton Club Lodge Drag Ball in the 1920s
and 1930s; Judy Garland, dressed in a tuxedo, thrilled
viewers as she danced with Gene Kelly in the 1950

film *Summer Stock*; and at this year's MTV Video
Music Awards, Madonna emerged from a wedding
cake in black tuxedo jacket, top hat and tall boots.
Almost as long as the tuxedo has been around, there
have been women to wear it, whether as lovers
or as entertainers or simply as pranksters like the
legendary young tobacco heir Griswold Lorillard and
his friends, who were said to have cut the tails off
their jackets to create the first tuxedos at the autumn
ball in Tuxedo Park, in 1886.

ACTRESS FRANCES WILLIAMS
IN "BROADWAY THROUGH A KEYHOLE," 1933
PHOTOGRAPH BY JOHN SPRINGER. JOHN SPRINGER COLLECTION/CORBIS

ACTRESS JANE WITHERS TAP DANCING, CA. 1935
PHOTOGRAPH BY JOHN SPRINGER. JOHN SPRINGER COLLECTION/CORBIS

MADONNA SINGING IN TOP HAT AND TUXEDO, 1993
PHOTOGRAPH BY NEAL PRESTON. CORBIS

fig.6

MODEL CARMEN DELL'OREFICE IN A BLACK ANDRE VAN PEIR TUXEDO.
PHOTOGRAPH BY NORMAN PARKINSON, CA. 1982.
NORMAN PARKINSON LIMITED/FIONA COWAN/CORBIS

fig.7

MODELS IN THE ROME APARTMENT OF CY TWOMBLY, WEARING LONG WHITE EVENING SUITS BY VALENTINO.
PEARL AND LACE DETAILS ORNAMENT THE CUFFS. THE SHOES ARE BY ROSETTI FOR VALENTINO.
THE MAN'S SUIT FEATURES A WHITE PAJAMA EMBROIDERED WAISTCOAT.
A MARBLE ROMAN HEAD, DRAWINGS BY TWOMBLY, AND ROCOCO CHAISES FRAME THE MODELS.
PHOTOGRAPH BY HENRY CLARKE, CA. 1968. CONDÉ NAST ARCHIVE/CORBIS

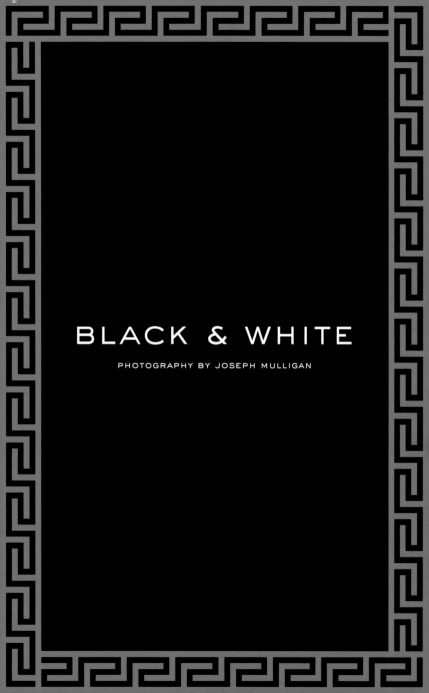

BLACK & WHITE

PHOTOGRAPHY BY JOSEPH MULLIGAN

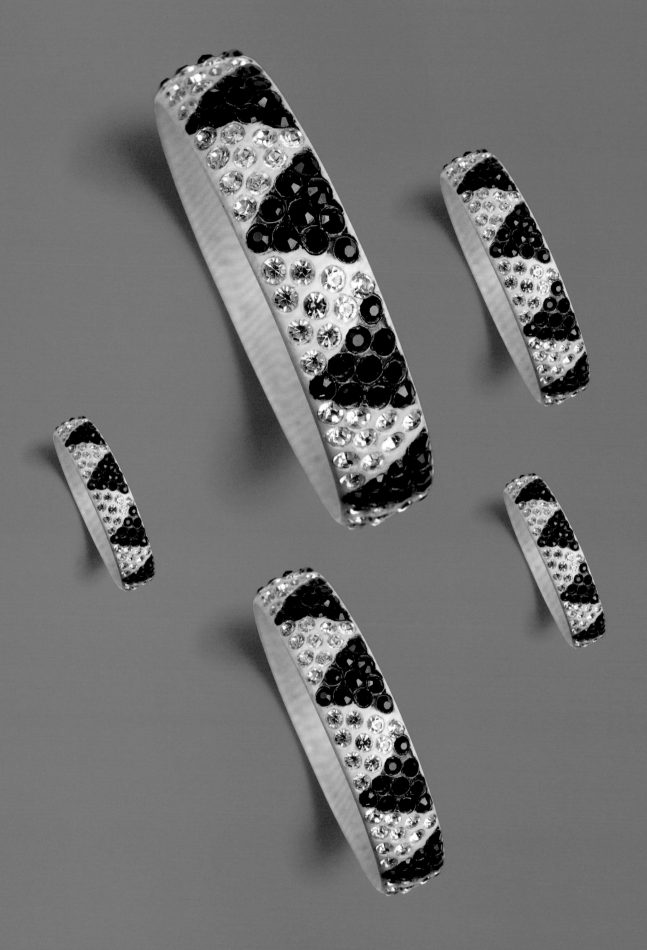

PLATE II.

PLATE III.

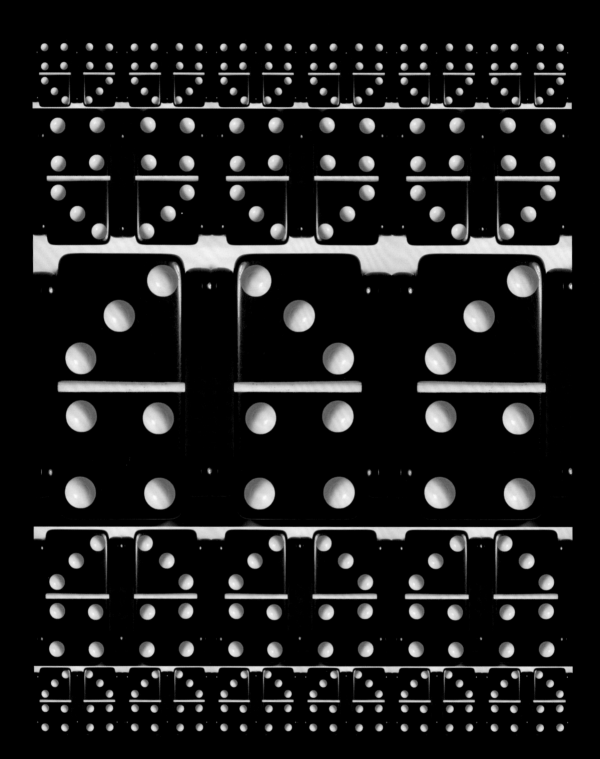

PLATE IV.

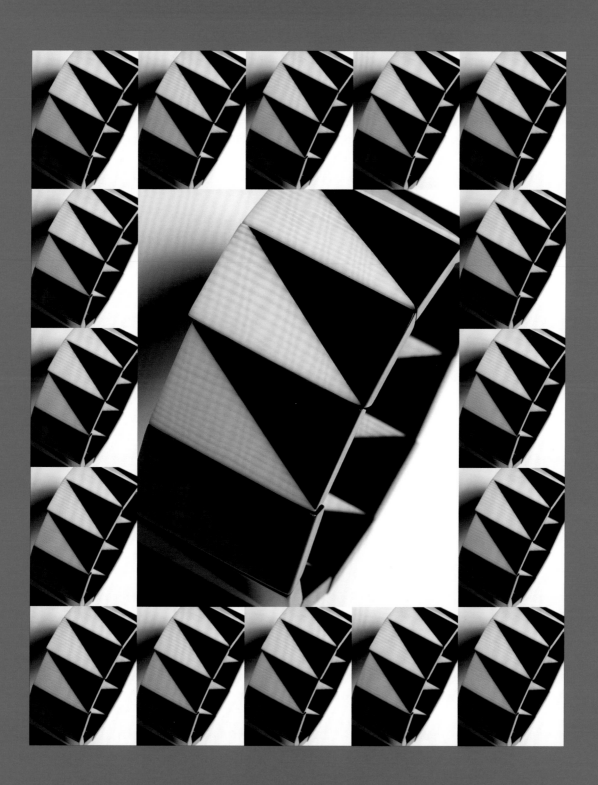

PLATE V.

PLATE VI.

BAKELITE

CREAM AND FRENCH IVORY BAKELITE PURSES, 1920—1950

PHOTOGRAPHY BY JOSEPH MULLIGAN

PLATE VII.

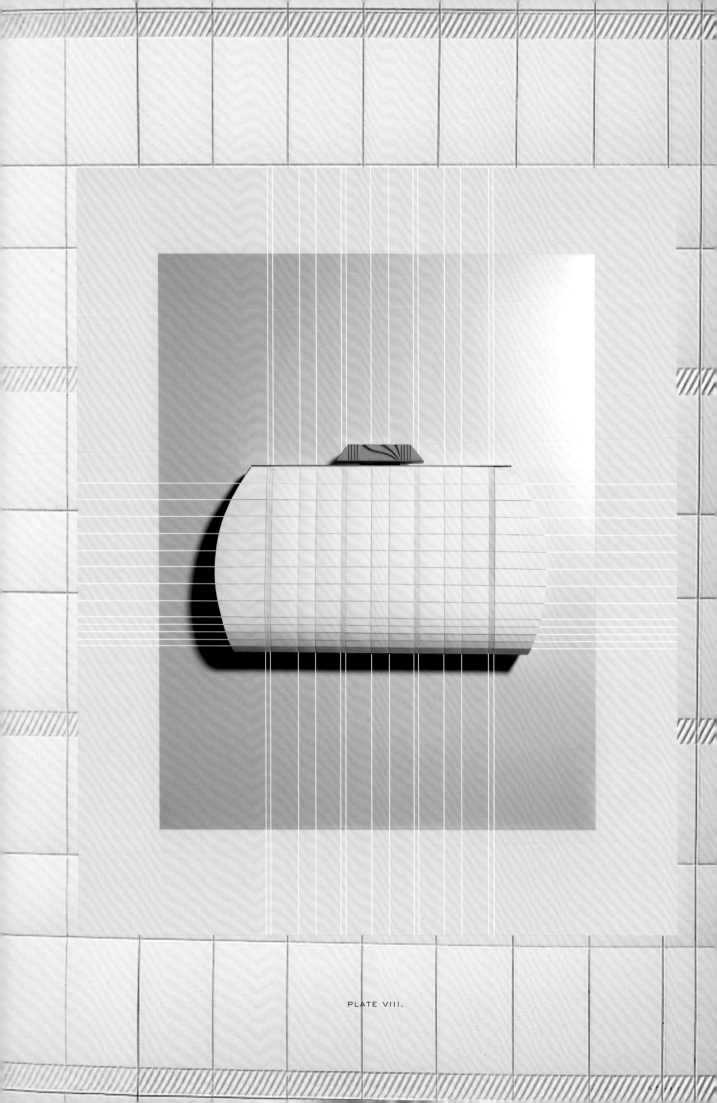

PLATE VIII.

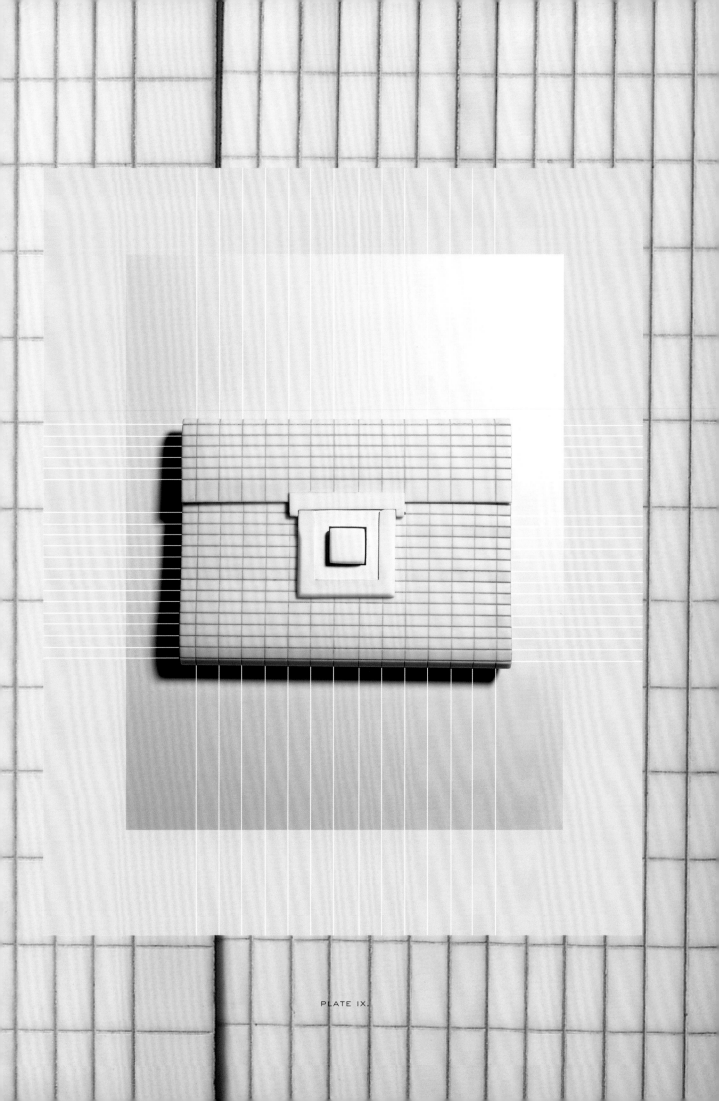

PLATE IX.

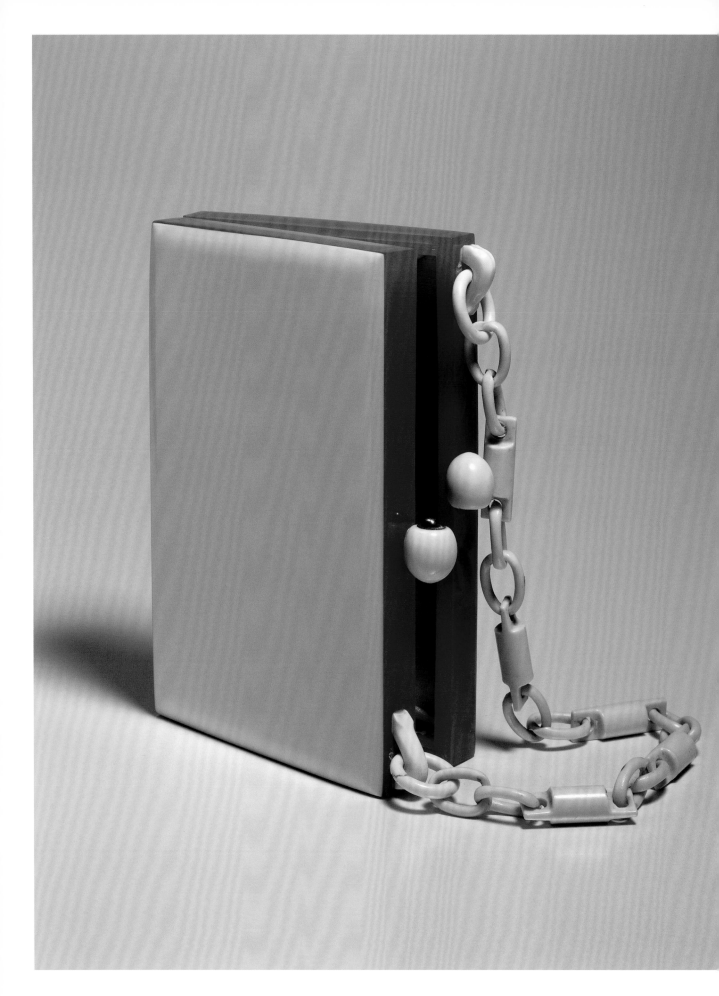

PLATE X.

PLATE XI.

fig. 8

PHOTOGRAPHY BY JEAN PIGOZZI, 2003

fig.9

fig. 10

fig.11

fig. 12

EARLY 19TH C. PARIS PORCELAIN COFFEE SERVICE; DALVA BROTHERS, INC.
PHOTOGRAPH BY JOSEPH MULLIGAN

DESCENT

PHOTOGRAPHY BY SHAUL SCHWARZ
TEXT BY NANCY DALVA

THE SOFTNESS OF

FLESH AND THE HARDNESS

OF STAIRS

COLLIDE AND COLLUDE

IN VERTIGINOUS

SPACE:

DESCENT

BY NOEMI LAFRANCE.

CLOCK TOWER,

THE CITY COURT BUILDING,

IN DOWNTOWN

NEW YORK.

PETER THE GREAT

PHOTOGRAPHY BY CHRISTIAN WITKIN

TEXT BY NANCY DALVA

CHOREOGRAPHER WENDY PERRON'S THE MAN AND THE ECHO IS A STUDY — A KIND OF PORTRAIT, BUT ONE THAT DELVES BENEATH THE SURFACE — OF AND FOR THE DANCER PETER BOAL. IN THE THEATER (AND IN THESE PHOTOS) YOU SEE THE SIGNATURE CALLIGRAPHIC GESTURES OF A POSTMODERNIST DRAWN BY A BRED-IN-THE-BONE CLASSICIST. AS A PRINCIPAL WITH THE NEW YORK CITY BALLET AND A TEACHER AT THE SCHOOL OF AMERICAN BALLET, BOAL DEFINES THE DANSEUR NOBLE. HE IS A PRINCE, A GOD, A KING. BUT HERE — DRESSED IN THAT MOST PEDESTRIAN OF GARMENTS, A BUSINESS SUIT — HE'S A RENEGADE. (PERRON HAS BROKEN IN, BOAL HAS BROKEN OUT.) THIS DANCE FITS HIM LIKE A SECOND SKIN, TO GET UNDERNEATH YOURS.

fig. 13

fig. 13

BLACK EVENING GOWN BY GEOFFREY BEENE, 2002
PHOTOGRAPHY BY JAY ZUKERKORN

fig.14

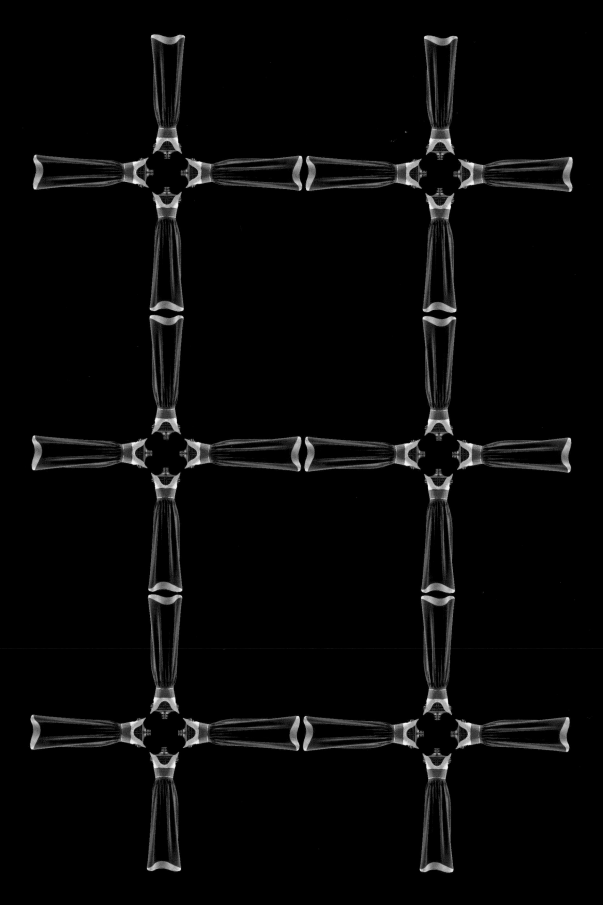

fig.14

BLACK EVENING GOWN BY GEOFFREY BEENE, 2002

MARIA CALEGARI

BART COOK

LOVE IN 3/4

PHOTOGRAPHY BY CHRISTIAN WITKIN

TEXT BY NANCY DALVA

MARIA CALEGARI AND BART COOK, MARRIED TO THEIR ART AND MARRIED TO EACH OTHER, MET AS MEMBERS OF THE NEW YORK CITY BALLET, WHERE EACH DANCED FOR MORE THAN TWENTY YEARS. THEIR CUPIDS WERE GEORGE BALANCHINE AND JEROME ROBBINS. TODAY THE DANSEUR NOBLE, WHO SERVED ROBBINS AS AN ASSISTANT BALLET MASTER AND WHO IS HIMSELF A CHOREOGRAPHER, AND HIS BEAUTIFUL RED-HEADED WIFE, WHO HEADS HER OWN SCHOOL IN CONNECTICUT, BOTH WORK AS RÉPÉTITEURS FOR THE BALANCHINE TRUST. TOGETHER AND SEPARATELY THEY TRAVEL THE WORLD, TEACHING THE WONDERFUL WORKS THEY DANCED SO WELL. (SHE A MARVEL OF MYSTICAL FEMININITY, HE A MARVEL OF MANLY CLARITY.) HERE YOU SEE THEM UNITED AFTER SIX WEEKS APART, CELEBRATING THEIR REUNION WITH A WALTZ. *I KISS YOUR HAND*, SAYS HE. SAYS SHE, *THAT BEARD!*

MARIA CALEGARI WITH HER STUDENTS: BETHANY BARTKUS, HALEY BILLINGS, ELIZABETH COX, JILLIAN KAPLITA, MORGAN MCEWEN, TEEGAN OGIELA, JILLIAN SAWYER

HAIR: FRED VAN DE BUNT FOR NUBEST AND CO. SALON, MAKEUP: FERIDE USLU FOR USLUAIRLINES.COM

RE-DRESSING POWER

THE ART OF YINKA SHONIBARE

As if an inventor of his own time-machine Yinka Shonibare stages elaborately realized tableaux that reinterpret eighteenth- and nineteenth-century art and history. Although his work is diverse, employing photography, painting, and film, it is his grand installations—populated by costumed figures—that have garnered the most acclaim for their deft blending of stagecraft, costume, and gesture. Working with a team of British-based theater and costume designers, Shonibare functions as something of a writer, director, and choreographer of his productions. He is as attentive to the craft and style of these pieces as a traditional couturier.

Simultaneously funny, beautiful, and barbed, Shonibare's art history clothes European traditions in African dress. The protagonists of his environments are usually clad in distinctively patterned textiles associated with Africa. An adaptation of Jean-Honoré Fragonard's *Swing (1767)* presents a lush environment for a headless swinging beauty. In Shonibare's construction, however, the viewer is now privy to the same view (up the woman's billowing dress) that Fragonard originally assigned to her lover's vantage point from the tangle of bushes in the foreground. His life-size tableaux based on Thomas Gainsborough's *Mr. and Mrs. Andrews (1748–49)* entitled, *Mr. and Mrs. Andrews without Their Heads (1998)*, gives us the trappings of the aristocracy, and slyly omits their heads. In the world that Shonibare deconstructs gesture, pose, fashion, and furniture carry identity far more than faces and minds. He presents a hybridized vision of art history with an amused, critical, and Technicolor adaptation of his sources.

Born in Britain, Shonibare moved with his parents to Nigeria as an infant and returned to London as a teenager. Educated in Nigeria and the United Kingdom, he received an advanced art degree from the conceptually-oriented and theory-driven Goldsmiths College in London. Echoing his hybrid cultural heritage, the textiles that are the lingua franca of Shonibare's work have a complex relationship to African identity.

fig. 13

THE SWING (AFTER FRAGONARD), 2001
DUTCH WAX PRINTED COTTON TEXTILE, LIFE-SIZE MANNEQUIN, SWING, ARTIFICIAL FOLIAGE
COLLECTION TATE BRITAIN

The bold patterns and dense coloration of the fabric, sometimes referred to as Dutch Wax, is popular in Africa, and is often worn in other parts of the world to signify Afro-centric allegiance. However the fabric uses techniques derived from traditional Indonesian batik and, because of Holland's colonial relationship to Indonesia, production of the fabric flourished in the Netherlands.

Most of these fabrics are still produced in Holland, even though their principle markets are in Africa. Shonibare uses Dutch Wax for his figurative sculptures, but he also paints on the cloth as an alternative to European traditions of painting on canvas. Within the fabric a complex history is woven, paralleling the African diaspora and the traditions that link Africa, Europe, and North America. It strongly recalls African culture, but is itself culturally hybrid, rather than "authentic." And, not incidentally, its also breathtakingly beautiful: Shonibare's virtuosity at combining these patterns and colors is astonishing.

The critical edge of his work has engaged territory outside of the art historical canon, as in his recent piece titled *Scramble for Africa*. Referring to the Berlin conference of 1884–1885, in which Africa was divided between five colonial powers for trade purposes, Shonibare's *Scramble* gathers fourteen life-size headless participants—dressed in Victorian men's suits—around a table whose surface features an inlay map of Africa. The table and its conferees hover like a spaceship on an elevated plinth, with light emanating from the base. The project provides a "fly on the wall" perspective as the figures dramatically gesticulate and negotiate for their share of Africa. In Shonibare's version the headless figures may allude to the fact that powerful members of the aristocracy often had their heads removed, or, as in other pieces, that his work is more concerned with the representation of power, not necessarily of the particular individuals who wield it. As his artistic practice evolves into new media (he is beginning work on a film), Shonibare will find new and provocative ways of redressing power. LAURIE ANN FARRELL

fig. 14

BIG BOY, 2002
WAX-PRINTED COTTON FABRIC, FIBREGLASS
COLLECTION SUSAN AND LEWIS MANILOW, CHICAGO

fig. 15

HOUND, 2000
FIBREGLASS DOGS AND FOX, DUTCH WAX PRINTED COTTON TEXTILE, LIFE-SIZE MANNEQUINS
COLLECTION OF EILEEN AND PETER NORTON

fig. 16

MR. AND MRS. ANDREWS WITHOUT THEIR HEADS, 1998
WAX-PRINT COTTON COSTUMES ON ARMATURES, DOG, LIFE-SIZE MANNEQUINS, BENCH, GUN
COLLECTION NATIONAL GALLERY OF CANADA

fig. 1

DANCE WITH ME

PHOTOGRAPHY BY JOSEF ASTOR

TEXT BY NANCY DALVA

ROB BESSERER IS THE PERFECT PARTNER, POSSESSED OF ALL THE FORMAL MANLY VIRTUES AND THEIR ALLURING CONTRASTS. STEADFAST BUT MYSTERIOUS; HANDSOME BUT MODEST; COURTLY BUT SEDUCTIVE; RELIABLE BUT THRILLING. WHENEVER HE DANCES, WE IMAGINE OURSELVES INTO HIS ARMS. HERE OUR STAND-IN IS MARJORIE FOLKMAN, AND WE COULDN'T ASK FOR ANYTHING MORE. THEY ARE FRED AND GINGER. THEY ARE BOGEY AND BACALL. HE'S GARY COOPER AND SHE'S BARBARA STANWYCK. HE'S CARY GRANT, AND YOU'RE YOU.

STYLIST: RON LOESCH, HAIR/MAKEUP: KATRINA BORGSTROM. BLACK TAFFETA SKIRT BY ROCHAS. TUXEDO BY HUGO BOSS. CUSTOM EMBROIDERY.

BOLEROS BY GEOFFREY BEENE, 2003–2004

PHOTOGRAPHY BY JAY ZUKERKORN

SPEAKING BALLET

PHOTOGRAPHY BY CHRISTIAN WITKIN

TEXT BY NANCY DALVA

BALLET IS A FORMAL LANGUAGE, WITH AN ALPHABET OF POSITIONS AND STEPS THAT CAN VARY FROM COUNTRY TO COUNTRY, COMPANY TO COMPANY, SCHOOL TO SCHOOL. CHOREOGRAPHERS, ESPECIALLY GREAT ONES, ALSO HAVE THEIR OWN DISTINCTIVE STYLES. THE DANCERS YOU SEE HERE, FOR EXAMPLE, SPEAK FLUENT BALANCHINE. ALL DANCE IN THE COMPANY HE FOUNDED, THE NEW YORK CITY BALLET. HERE, THOUGH, THEY ARE SPEAKING SOMETHING NEW, AS ALBERT EVANS, AN NYCB PRINCIPAL, STEPS OUT ON HIS OWN AS A CHOREOGRAPHER, AND JANIE TAYLOR AND SÉBASTIEN MARCOVICI JOIN HIM IN A CLASSICAL CONVERSATION DEVISED FOR US.

fig.18

THE TWO STUDENTS, 2001

FORMAL SITTING

THE PHOTOGRAPHS OF TINA BARNEY

When Isabel Archer, the protagonist of *The Portrait of a Lady*, and easily the most fascinating and inquisitive of Henry James's beautiful American heroines, first encounters the British on her travels abroad, she is consumed with curiosity. She may not be the first, and certainly is not the last, to suffer the pangs of an independent democratic spirit in the midst of British teatime, but she is beautiful in her boldness, at once innocent and dogmatic. Questions arise about the English character, the state of politics, the manners and customs of the royal family, the peculiarities of the aristocracy. How, she wonders, do they manage to sit and stand without seeming to?

Tina Barney is an Isabel of a different sort. For almost thirty years she has constructed a critique of patrician otherness in photographs made in rambling New England beach houses and New York apartments. Thanks to her, we've gotten used to pushing our way into exclusive backyard barbecues and enormous living rooms busy with decorator wallpaper and the odd masterpiece by Degas on the wall. Now we're off on the Grand Tour. To British public school no less, where the boys look like Princes William and Henry and the girls…well, the girls must wear uniforms that are no match for vests and frock coats. Away from flesh and blue blood, in her European series (which includes the Italian and the French as well as the British), Barney acts as both guide and supplicant: "Would you, could you, please stand there for a minute?" In choosing to interpret a culture of which she is not a part, she, like her Jamesian prototype, has been not only courageous but also innovative. There is something so wonderfully off about the design of these photographs that the candid rhetoric Barney is known for takes an eccentric leap, adding color and space itself to the cast of characters. Along with the ability to sit and stand without seeming to, she has given us something else to arouse our wonder about the British as well as photography. MERRY FORESTA

fig. 19

THE DINING HALL, 2001

*fig.*20

THE SCHOOLGIRLS, 2001

fig.21

THE LOLLIPOPS, 2001

fig.23

FAIRMONT HOTEL, DALLAS, TEXAS, 2001
PHOTOGRAPH BY MICHELE TECCO

*fig.*24

PENNSYLVANIA CARWASH, 2002
PHOTOGRAPH BY MICHELE TECCO

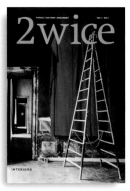

Feet vol 1 : no 1
SOLD OUT

Laura Jacobs, Georges Bataille, Rosalind Krauss, RoseLee Goldberg, Nancy Dalva, Valerie Steele, Linda O'Keefe, and Footsucker author Geoff Nicholson. Photographers include Josef Astor, Lillian Bassman, Andrew Eccles, Timothy Greenfield-Sanders, Horst, Nina Leen, Graham MacIndoe, Arno Rafael Minkkinen, Martin Munkacsi, Richard Ross, and James Wojcik.

Interiors vol 1 : no 2
SOLD OUT

Rick Poynor on shelter magazines, Richard B. Woodward on brothels, William Harris on painter Paul Winstanley, Nancy Dalva on interiority, playwright John Jesurun, and Donald Albrecht on movie studios. Photographers include Robert Polidori, Duane Michals, Timothy Hursley, Jean Pigozzi, Lorna Bieber, Craig Kalpakjian, Richard Barnes, Tomoko Yoneda, John Dugdale, Jean Kallina, and Adam Bartos.

Self vol 2 : no 1
AVAILABLE US$22.00

Dr. Ian Wilmut on cloning, Dr. David Haig, Lewis Black, Nancy Dalva, John Kelly, Tennessee Williams, and Garth Fagan. Interviews with Maya Angelou, the Ganz twins, and Julia Mandle. Photographers include Marvin Newman, Susan Derges, Lee Friedlander, Marcia Lippman, and Jean Pigozzi.

Uniform vol 2 : no 2
AVAILABLE US$22.00

Richard Martin on militarism, Alison Maddex on Playboy bunnies, Laura Jacobs on stewardesses, Arthur Golden on kimonos, Mark Wigley on lawns, Rick Poynor on Muzak, Steven Heller on doormen. Interviews with Annette Meyer, The Art Guys, Todd Oldham, and Karen Kimmel. Photographers Marcia Lippman, Graham MacIndoe, Jeff Riedl, Josef Sudek, Christian Witkin, and James Wojcik.

Night vol 3 : no 1
AVAILABLE US$22.00

Nightwalker by Louis Aragon, Richard Martin on the little black dress, Joan Acocella on Bob Fosse, Anne Wilkes Tucker on Brassaï, Karrie Jacobs on Brasília. Photographers Michael Ackerman, Brassaï, Todd Eberle, Todd Hido, Kate Orné, Jean Pigozzi, Tom Pritchard, Edward Quinn, Peter Rad, Lynn Saville, Ross T. Smith, Mark Steinmetz, Edel Verzijl, and Jay Zukerkorn.

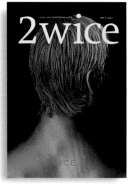

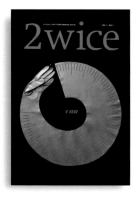

The End vol 3 : no 2
AVAILABLE US$22.00

Interviews with filmmaker Don McKellar and designers Laurene Leon and Constantin Boym, artist Charles Long, humorist Bruce McCall, miniature forensics, curtain calls, and fashion designer Hussein Chalayan. Photographers include Jerry Dantzic, Dan Winters, Marcus Tomlinson, Jean Kallina, and Dafna Shalom.

Spring vol 4 : no 1
AVAILABLE US$22.00

Choreographers David Parker, Ronald K. Brown, Molissa Fenley, Stephen Petronio, and dancer Foofwa D'Imobilite. Fiction by Jimmy Gleacher, tribute to Richard Martin, the Periodic Breakfast Table, illustrator Barbara Schwinn-Jordan, Meiji kimono designs. Photographers include Martin Schoeller, Josef Astor, Nelson Bakerman, Stephen Gill, Paula Horn Kotis, Brigitte Lacombe, and Christian Witkin.

Ice vol 4 : no 2
SOLD OUT

Choreographer Paul Taylor, Wilson Bentley's snowflake studies, Hitchcock's ice blondes, dancers Tom Gold and Banu Ogan, Elizabeth David on the history of ice and food, cryogenics, and ice carving. Artist Marc Quinn and photographers William Eggleston, Stuart Klipper, Andrew Eccles, Anders Overgaard, Gary Braasch, Larry Gianettino, Jean Pigozzi, Peter Basch, and John Halpern.

Camera vol 5 : no 1
AVAILABLE US$22.00

Choreographers Twyla Tharp and Karole Armitage, performer John Kelly, and playwright John Jesurun. James Wolcott on Minox cameras, Rick Poynor on the Lomo camera, Laura Jacobs' recollection of a Zeiss microscope, Tobi Tobias on Twiggy. Photographers Richard Barnes, Andrew Eccles, Stephen Gill, Arnold Odermatt, Martin Parr, Jean Pigozzi, Martin Schoeller, Richard Torchia, and Jay Zukerkorn.

Car vol 5 : no 2
AVAILABLE US$22.00

Essays by Judith Hoos Fox, Lucy Flint-Gohlke, David Frankel, Greil Marcus, James Wolcott, Paul Arthur, Giuliana Bruno, Tobi Tobias, and Phil Patton. Artists include Matthew Barney, Adam Bartos, Andrew Bush, Sophie Calle, Nan Goldin, Joseph Mulligan, Daniel Storto, and Andrea Zittel.

Picnic vol 6 : no 1
AVAILABLE US$22.00

Photography by Martin Schoeller, Christian Witkin, Tony Rinaldo, Sarah Blodgett, Anita Calero, Sally Mann, Laura Kleger, Joseph Mulligan, and Jean Pigozzi. Texts by Donald Albrecht, Maya Angelou, Nancy Dalva, Henry Louis Gates, Jr., Charles Simic, and Tobi Tobias. Performances by Merce Cunningham, Mark Morris, Jamie Bishton, and Alexandre Proia.

Glow vol 6 : no 2
AVAILABLE US$22.00

Artists include Michael Flomen, Stephen Hendee, Amanda Means, Taku Satoh, Peter Garfield, Andrew Moore, Susan Wides, Max Becher and Andrea Robbins. Texts by Darsie Alexander, Dietrich Neumann, Russell Flinchum, Shonquis and, Tobi Tobias.

Animal vol 7 : no 1
AVAILABLE US$22.00

Artists include Alen MacWeeney, Michael O'Neill, Richard Barnes, Dwight Eschliman, Sandra Raredon, Arne Svenson, Larry Gianettino, Chip Simons, Tamara Staples. Texts by Laura Jacobs on animals in choreography, Andy Grundberg, and Randi Mates. Performances by the Paul Taylor Dance Company, the Parsons Dance Company, Alexandre Proia, and the Stephen Petronio Dance Company.

2wice

VISUAL AND PERFORMING ARTS
VOLUME 7 NUMBER 2

EDITOR IN CHIEF
Patsy Tarr

EDITOR / DESIGNER
Abbott Miller

DESIGN ASSOCIATE
Jeremy Hoffman
Pentagram

MANAGING EDITOR
Jane Rosch

EDITORIAL ASSOCIATE
Jess Mackta

SENIOR EDITOR /
WRITER
Nancy Dalva

NEW MEDIA
Jeff Tarr, Jr.

2WICE ASSOCIATE
Jennifer D. Tarr

FOUNDATION
ADMINISTRATOR
Michael Bloom

CONTRIBUTING EDITOR,
DANCE
Phil Sandstrom

ADVISORY BOARD
Karole Armitage
Geoffrey Beene
André Bishop
Jamie Bishton
Trisha Brown
Rika Burnham
Maria Calegari
Elaine Lustig Cohen
Bart Cook
Merce Cunningham
Julie Dale
Leon Dalva
James Danziger
Douglas Dunn
Molissa Fenley
Audrey Friedman
Henry Louis Gates, Jr.
Dorothy Globus
Neil Greenberg
Barbara Horgan
John Jesurun
John Kelly
Wendy Keys
Harold Koda
Salvatore La Rosa
Kevin MacKenzie
Peter Martins
Ariel Meyerowitz

Mark Morris
Gregory Mosher
Alan Moss
David Parsons
Patricia Pastor
Richard Peña
Stephen Petronio
Jean Pigozzi
C. Thibaud Pomerantz
Etheleen Staley
Elizabeth Streb
Paul Taylor
Twyla Tharp
Robert Wilson
Taki Wise

2WICE
2wice® is published by the
2wice Arts Foundation, Inc.
Financial support is derived
from individual, corporate,
and foundation contributions
and reader subscriptions.

2wice Arts Foundation, Inc.,
is a tax-exempt organization
under section 501(c)(3) of
the Internal Revenue Code.
Contributions to the 2wice
Arts Foundation, Inc., are
tax-deductible to the extent
provided by law.

ACKNOWLEDGMENTS
Kirsten MacDonald Bennett,
Patrick Busse, Andrew
DeMattos, Dawn Goodrich,
Kathy Hall, Jamie Mandell
Hoffman, Ruth Janson,
Johnschen Kudos, Ellen
Lupton, Mike McKillips,
Larry McNiece, Fred Paul,
Leslie Powell, Diane
Raimondo, Silke Ronneburg,
Scheufelen North America

PRINTED IN THE U.S.
Peake Printers, Inc.
2500 Schuster Drive,
Cheverly, MD 20781

SUBSCRIPTION
INFORMATION
One year (two issues)
$40 U.S. $48 FOREIGN

To subscribe or to make
changes to an existing
subscription, please visit our
website at www.2wice.org
or contact us at:

2wice Arts Foundation
145 Central Park West
New York, NY 10023
Phone: 866 88 2WICE
Fax: 866 FX 2WICE
Email: info@2wice.org

FRONT COVER
Detail of hands, Baroque
Dance Ensemble, photo-
graph by Christian Witkin

ISBN 0-9723886-2-1
© 2004 2wice
All Rights Reserved

SUBSCRIBE

NAME

TEL

ADDRESS

CITY

STATE

ZIP

COUNTRY

EMAIL

GIFT SUBSCRIPTION

FROM

TEL

EMAIL

MESSAGE

○ I YEAR U.S. $40   ○ I YEAR FOREIGN $48

○ AUTOMATIC RENEWAL

○ CHECK PAYABLE TO 2WICE ARTS FOUNDATION

○ MASTERCARD   ○ VISA   ○ AMEX

CARD NO.

EXP. DATE

SIGNATURE

Fax subscription form to:
866 FX 2WICE
631 907 8985

Or subscribe online at
www.2wice.org

For subscriptions outside
North America, contact:

Bruil & van de Staaij
Postbus 75
7940 AB MEPPEL
The Netherlands
P +31 522 261 303
F +31 522 257 827
info@bruil.info
www.bruil.info

AWARDS

TYPE DIRECTORS CLUB
JUDGE'S CHOICE
2002

ART DIRECTORS CLUB
GOLD MEDAL
2004

ART DIRECTORS CLUB
DISTINCTION
2004

AIGA 365
EXCELLENCE
2003 2001

TOKYO TYPE
DIRECTORS CLUB
DESIGN
2004

SOCIETY OF
PUBLICATION DESIGNERS
MAGAZINE OF
THE YEAR
1998

SOCIETY OF
PUBLICATION DESIGNERS
GOLD MEDAL
2003 1998

I.D. DESIGN REVIEW
DISTINCTION
2004 1998

BRITISH DESIGN AND
ART DIRECTION AWARD
DESIGN
2000 1998

AMERICAN CENTER
FOR DESIGN'S 100 SHOW
DESIGN
2002 2000

SOCIETY OF
PUBLICATION DESIGNERS
MERIT
2002 2001 1999

BRNO COMPETITION
BEST MAGAZINE
2000

SOCIETY OF
PUBLICATION DESIGNERS
SILVER MEDAL
2001

ART DIRECTORS CLUB
DISTINCTIVE
MERIT
2001

ART DIRECTORS CLUB
DESIGN
2000

TYPE DIRECTORS CLUB
DESIGN
2000

CONTRIBUTORS

JOSEF ASTOR has published his photographs in *Vanity Fair*, *The New Yorker*, and *The New York Times Magazine*, among others. Astor is on the faculty of the School of Visual Arts and teaches in the MFA program at Bard College. He is currently working on a book of portraits and dance photography.

TINA BARNEY is a native New Yorker who currently lives in Rhode Island. Her photographs can be viewed at Janet Borden Inc.

LAURIE ANN FARRELL is curator at the Museum for African Art, New York. She writes on the subject of contemporary art from Africa and regularly contributes to *African Arts*, *Artthrob*, and *Nka: Journal of Contemporary African Art*.

MERRY FORESTA currently directs the Smithsonian Photography Initiative. Her most recent book is *At First Sight: Photography and the Smithsonian*.

CYNTHIA GREIG is a fine-art photographer and independent curator living in Bloomfield Hills, Michigan. She is coauthor of *Women in Pants: Manly Maidens, Cowgirls, and Other Renegades*, published recently by Harry N. Abrams.

ANDY GRUNDBERG is an art critic living in Washington, D.C., where he is the Chair of the Photography department at the Corcoran College of Art and Design. His writings on photography are collected in the book *Crisis of the Real* published by Aperture.

JOSEPH MULLIGAN is a New York-based photographer specializing in portraiture and still-life photography.

JEAN PIGOZZI was a photographer long before he became a venture capitalist. A native Parisian, he currently lives in Switzerland.

SHAUL SCHWARZ has published his photographs in *Life, Time, The New York Times, Paris Match, Le Monde II, L'Espresso*. Schwarz was born in Israel and has been represented by Corbis and based in New York since 1999.

YINKA SHONIBARE lives and works in London. His work has appeared in exhibitions worldwide, including the Tate Modern, PS1, the Studio Museum in Harlem, the Andy Warhol Museum, the Museum for African Art, and the Museum of Contemporary Art, Sydney.

CATHERINE SMITH is an artist, author, and collector of antique photographs living in Fenton, Michigan. She is coauthor of *Women in Pants: Manly Maidens, Cowgirls, and Other Renegades*, published recently by Harry N. Abrams.

ANDREW SOLOMON is the author of *The Irony Tower: Soviet Artists in a Time of Glasnost*; the novel *A Stone Boat*; and *The Noonday Demon: An Atlas of Depression*, which won the National Book Award in 2001 and was a finalist for the Pulitzer Prize in 2002. He lives in New York and London.

MICHELE TECCO is a photographer from Pennsylvania, currently living in Baltimore. She has exhibited at the Dallas Museum of Art, and the CAC in Aix-en-Provence, France.

PHILLIP TOLEDANO became a photographer after a ten-year career as an art director in advertising. His work has appeared in the *New York Times Magazine* and *Harper's Bazaar* among others. He is working on a book, *Bankrupt. Photographs of Recently Vacated Offices* to be published next fall.

CHRISTIAN WITKIN has published his photographs in numerous magazines, including *Vanity Fair, The New York Times Magazine, Surface*, and *Harper's Bazaar*. His photographs have been exhibited in New York, Amsterdam, and Tokyo, and his first book, *India: Photographs by Christian Witkin*, was published in 2003.

JAY ZUKERKORN'S still life photography is featured in advertising for Shiseido, Aveda, Lancome, Estee Lauder, and Gucci. His editorial clients include *Vogue, Harper's Bazaar, Men's Health*, and *Arude*.